DATE DUE

THE GATEWAY ARCH
Celebrating Western Expansion

by Joanne Mattern

RED
CHAIR
·PRESS·

Let's Celebrate America is produced and published by Red Chair Press:

Red Chair Press LLC   PO Box 333   South Egremont, MA 01258-0333

www.redchairpress.com

About the Author

Joanne Mattern is a former editor and the author of nearly 350 books for children and teens. She began writing when she was a little girl and just never stopped! Joanne loves nonfiction because she enjoys bringing history and science topics to life and showing young readers that nonfiction is full of compelling stories! Joanne lives in New York State with her husband, four children, and several pets.

Publisher's Cataloging-In-Publication Data

Names: Mattern, Joanne, 1963–

Title: The Gateway Arch : celebrating western expansion / by Joanne Mattern.

Description: South Egremont, MA : Red Chair Press, [2017] | Series: Let's celebrate America | Interest age level: 008-012. | Includes a glossary and references for additional reading. | "Core content classroom."--Cover. | Includes bibliographical references and index. | Summary: "This magnificent arch rises on the banks of the Mississippi River in St. Louis, Missouri. The nation's tallest monument is the centerpiece of the Jefferson National Expansion Memorial, honoring Thomas Jefferson's vision of westward expansion. Mired in controversy in the beginning, this amazing structure is now a national treasure and symbol of the nation's reach from the Atlantic to the Pacific."--Provided by publisher.

Identifiers: LCCN 2016954998 | ISBN 978-1-63440-228-6 (library hardcover) | ISBN 978-1-63440-238-5 (paperback) | ISBN 978-1-63440-248-4 (ebook)

Subjects: LCSH: Gateway Arch (Saint Louis, Mo.)--History--Juvenile literature. | Jefferson National Expansion Memorial (Saint Louis, Mo.)--Juvenile literature. | United States--Territorial expansion--Juvenile literature. | West (U.S.)--History--Juvenile literature. | CYAC: Gateway Arch (Saint Louis, Mo.)--History. | United States--Territorial expansion. | West (U.S.)--History.

Classification: LCC F474.S265 G38 2017 (print) | LCC F474.S265 (ebook) | DDC 977.8/66--dc23

Map illustrations by Joe LeMonnier

Photo credits: p. 9: American Philosophical Society; p. 12: Granger; cover, p. 1, 28, back cover: Ingimage; p. 7, 17, 25: Library of Congress; p. 13, 15: National Archives; p. 30, 31, 33: National Park Service; p. 3, 4, 5, 8, 9, 11, 29, 31: Shutterstock; p. 14, 17, 18, 19, 20, 21, 22, 23, 24, 25, 27: St. Louis Post-Dispatch

Printed in the United States of America
0517 1P WRZF17

Table of Contents

Heading West

The United States is a huge nation. When European settlers first came to this country, they settled along the eastern coast. As the years passed and the nation grew, settlers began heading west. This **migration** would change the nation.

Missouri pioneer homestead

During the 1800s, the United States changed in many ways. The United States claimed more land in the west. More people traveled west to start new lives. At first they traveled in covered wagons. Later, railroads made the trip easier. The United States was growing and changing.

Life in the West was very different from life in the East. Many Americans viewed the West as a special place. They wanted to honor the ways our nation grew. It took a very unusual **monument** to honor the western **frontier**. That monument is the Gateway Arch.

Pioneers traveled in covered wagons.

IT'S A FACT

The Gateway Arch is the tallest monument in the United States.

Land from France

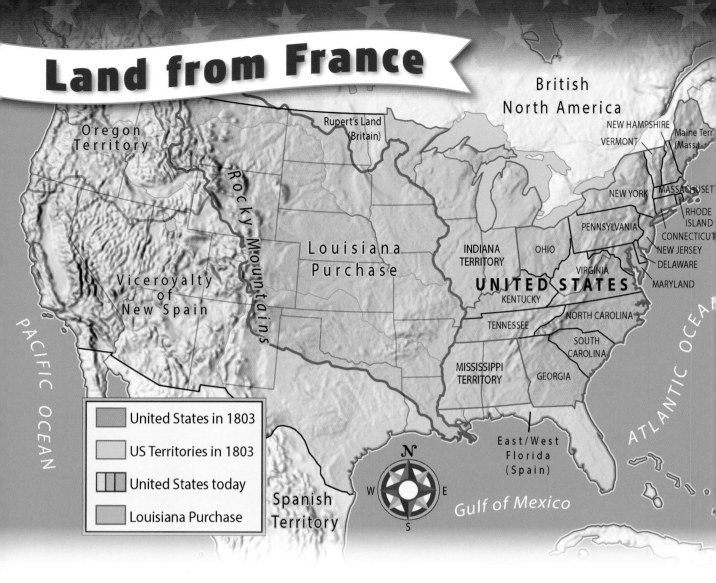

British North America

Oregon Territory

Rupert's Land (Britain)

NEW HAMPSHIRE
VERMONT
Maine Terr (Mass.)

NEW YORK
MASSACHUSET
RHODE ISLAND
PENNSYLVANIA
CONNECTICUT
NEW JERSEY
DELAWARE

Rocky Mountains

Louisiana Purchase

INDIANA TERRITORY
OHIO

Viceroyalty of New Spain

VIRGINIA
UNITED STATES
MARYLAND
KENTUCKY

TENNESSEE

NORTH CAROLINA

SOUTH CAROLINA

PACIFIC OCEAN

MISSISSIPPI TERRITORY
GEORGIA

ATLANTIC OCEAN

United States in 1803

US Territories in 1803

United States today

Louisiana Purchase

East/West Florida (Spain)

Spanish Territory

Gulf of Mexico

In 1803, the United States' western border was the Mississippi River. Then President Thomas Jefferson bought about 828,000 square miles of land from France. He did not even know what this part of North America was like. The price was $15 million dollars. The land stretched from the Mississippi River to the Rocky Mountains and from the Gulf of Mexico to Canada. This land was called the Louisiana Purchase.

President Jefferson sent James Monroe to France to negotiate the Louisiana Purchase. Jefferson told Monroe,

> **"All eyes, all hopes, are now fixed on you, for on the event of the mission depends the future destinies of this republic."**

The Louisiana Purchase almost doubled the size of the United States. President Jefferson wanted to know what this new land was like. He hired two men, Meriwether Lewis and William Clark, to explore the area. Lewis and Clark started their trip in St. Louis, Missouri in May 1804.

Meriwether Lewis

The two men and their team were called the Corps of Discovery. They spent two years exploring the wilderness. They traveled to North Dakota and then west to Oregon. Then they turned around and came home. When they arrived back in St. Louis in September 1806, a crowd of people greeted them with a huge celebration.

William Clark

New Discoveries

The Corps of Discovery made many amazing discoveries during their trip. William Clark made detailed maps of their journey. Settlers used these maps for many years as they traveled west. The men also kept journals. They wrote down everything they saw. They described high mountains, flat plains, and thick forests. The men wrote about and drew pictures of animals and plants no one in the East had ever seen. Thanks to Lewis and Clark, people in the East got their first look at grizzly bears, mule deer, prairie dogs, and more.

Lewis and Clark during their journey

Above: Journals from Lewis and Clark.
Right: Statue in North Dakota of Sacagawea

Lewis and Clark also met with Native Americans who were already living in the West. They told tribe leaders they were there in peace. They also promised the United States would trade with native tribes. Most of the tribes were friendly. One native woman named Sacagawea traveled with Lewis and Clark and helped them find their way in the new land.

The Gateway to the West

Lewis and Clark's trip created a trail to the West. Many people decided to follow that trail. Some wanted to start a new life by farming the new land. Others, such as fur trappers and traders, wanted to make money. In 1849, thousands traveled west to find gold in the Gold Rush. The starting point for most of these western trips was St. Louis. The city became the last place to buy supplies before settlers started on the long journey west. For this reason, St. Louis became known as the Gateway to the West.

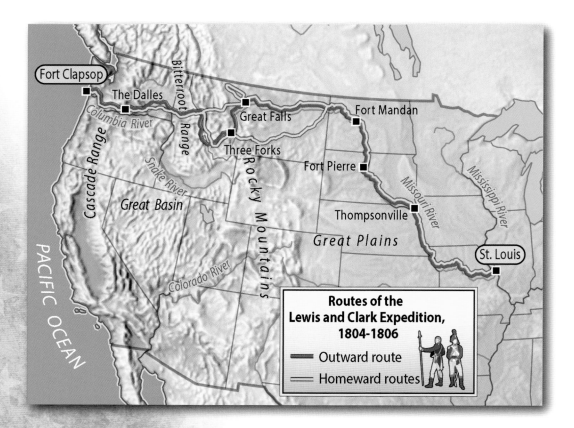

Beginning in 1841, settlers began traveling along the new Oregon Trail. This trail led from Missouri across the Great Plains and the Rocky Mountains to Oregon on the Pacific Coast. Part of the Oregon Trail covered the same route that Lewis and Clark took on their **expedition**. Between 1841 and 1860, more than 50,000 people crossed the United States on the Oregon Trail.

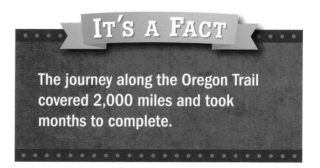

IT'S A FACT

The journey along the Oregon Trail covered 2,000 miles and took months to complete.

The Frontier Closes

There was so much land in the West that the U.S. government started giving it away. In 1862, the Homestead Act gave 160 acres of land to anyone who was 21 years of age or older. To keep the land, or homestead, the settler had to live on it and take care of it for five years. Thousands of people rushed west to take advantage of this offer. At least 400,000 people moved west over the next thirty years.

In 1890, the United States government counted how many people lived in the country. The total was 63 million people. The government also found out that so many people had settled in the West that there was no longer any free land. So the government declared that the frontier was closed.

Certificate of eligibility under the Homestead Act

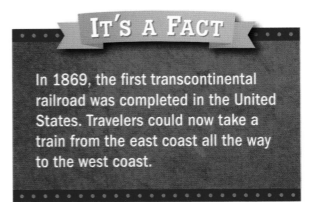

IT'S A FACT

In 1869, the first transcontinental railroad was completed in the United States. Travelers could now take a train from the east coast all the way to the west coast.

Honoring Westward Expansion

St. Louis had been a busy, successful city during the westward **expansion**. But after the frontier closed, things changed. By the 1930s, parts of the city were in bad shape. Buildings were empty and falling down. The waterfront was no longer busy. Instead it was a sad, lonely place.

St. Louis riverfront, before demolition began to clear land for the memorial

City leaders decided to change the waterfront. In 1933, Mayor Bernard Dickmann and a lawyer named Luther Ely Smith began to plan. They remembered that St. Louis had been called the Gateway to the West. They wanted to honor the explorers and settlers who traveled west and changed the nation forever. So they came

Bernard Dickmann

up with the idea of a monument that would honor Thomas Jefferson and his role in westward expansion. The **memorial** would also honor Lewis and Clark and their role in opening the West.

In 1935, Smith and Dickmann formed the Jefferson National Expansion Memorial Association, or JNEMA (or *Jenny May*). The JNEMA worked hard to raise money for the monument. The United States government and the city offered to pay for it. But then the United States fought in World War II from 1941 to 1945. The project was put on hold.

Finding an Architect

JNEMA got back to work after World War II ended. In 1947, the organization held a contest to pick a design for the monument. The **architect** who submitted the best design would win money and also get to plan the monument.

JNEMA received 172 entries in the contest. Everyone agreed that the best design came from an architect named Eero Saarinen. Saarinen called for a 630-foot-tall arch made of stainless steel and concrete. The arch would soar over the Mississippi River. It would be **hollow** inside so visitors could travel to the top. The design became known as the Gateway Arch because it looked like a gateway to the West.

Eero Saarinen was born in Finland on August 10, 1910. His family moved to the United States when he was twelve years old. Saarinen's father was also an architect. He taught his children to draw, design, and work hard at whatever job they did. Saarinen designed many buildings around the United States. He died in 1961, and never got to see the Gateway Arch completed.

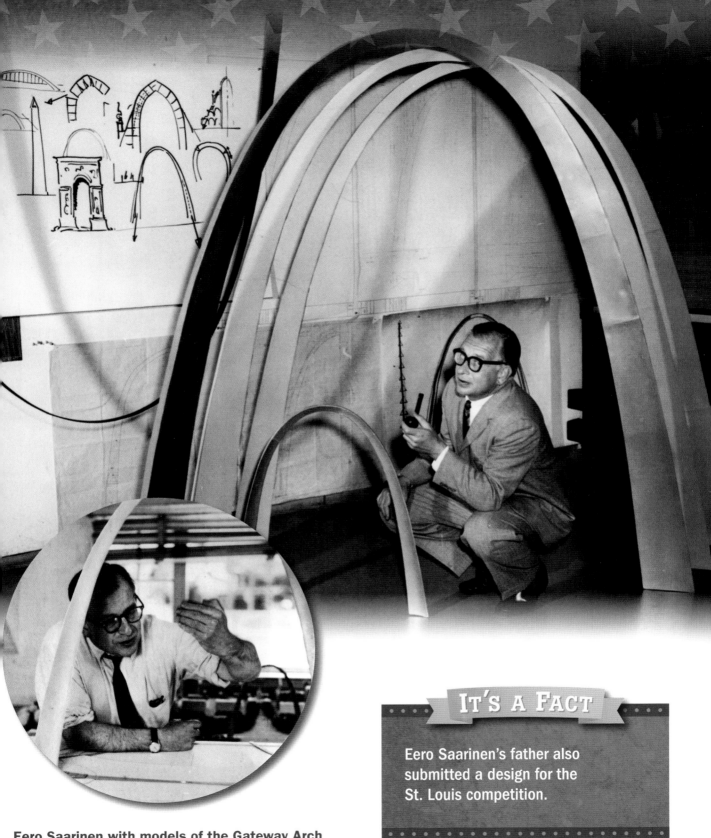

Eero Saarinen's father also submitted a design for the St. Louis competition.

Eero Saarinen with models of the Gateway Arch

17

Digging Deep

Workers demolish a building, one of the first to be razed for the memorial.

The city of St. Louis tore down some buildings along the waterfront to clear the land to build the monument. President Harry S. Truman **dedicated** the site on June 10, 1950. But before work could begin, the United States entered the Korean War. The U.S. fought in that war until 1953. During that time, there was no **federal** money to build the Arch.

After the war ended, there were even more delays. The city of St. Louis had to move a set of railroad tracks that were located along the river. This took several years. Finally, in 1961, workers began digging the Arch's **foundations**.

The Arch had to be built on deep foundations to hold up the weight of the monument. Workers blasted through 60 feet of dirt and rocks to dig two huge holes. The bottoms of the foundation rest on solid **bedrock**. Then workers poured concrete into the holes to create the foundation.

Workers pour concrete into the north leg of the memorial.

The Arch Takes Shape

Two years after the foundations were dug, workers began building the Arch in 1963. They stacked steel blocks on top of each other. Each block was shaped like a triangle. The largest blocks were placed on the bottom of the structure. The blocks got smaller in size as they moved up the Arch. The smallest blocks would be placed on top. Steel bands held the blocks together. A stainless steel shell covered the outside.

Workers at the north leg

IT'S A FACT

The Gateway Arch weighs 17,246 tons.

There are 142 blocks in the Arch.

Building the arch was dangerous work. Usually, workers use a **scaffold** when they work high off the ground. However, the size and shape of the Arch meant that a scaffold could not be used. Instead, workers stood on the Arch itself. Special machines called creeper derricks moved up and down the Arch on a track. These derricks carried materials to the workers high above.

The wind made the arches move. People worried that a worker would be blown right off! People also worried that the Arch might collapse. Each leg of the Arch had to support its own weight plus the weight of the workers and their equipment. In spite of the danger, no workers were killed or badly injured.

Inside the Arch

Workers were busy inside the hollow legs of the Arch as well as on the outside. They built a staircase inside each leg. They also put in electric lines and lights.

The Arch was designed so that visitors could travel up each leg to an observation deck on the top. Most monuments have elevators to take visitors up, but this would not work on an arch, because of the curved structure and the fact that the base was much bigger than the top. Finally, a man named Richard Bowser came up with the answer. Bowser designed a **tram** with separate cars like the seats on a Ferris wheel. Each car's door is only four and a half feet wide. Each side of the arch has its own tram. A tram has eight cars, and each car holds eight people.

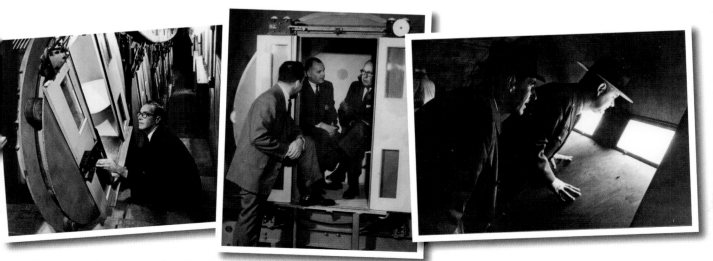

Left: An engineer checks the tram doors.
Center: Inside the tram car
Right: Enjoying the view from the top

The Last Piece

Both sides of the Arch were built at the same time. The plan was that the two sides would meet at the top. However, architects and workers were not sure this plan would work. The legs of the Arch were so heavy that they sagged in the middle. Workers solved this problem by putting a metal support between the Arch to keep the legs in place.

Another problem was the heat and the cold. The steel in the Arch expanded, or got bigger, when it got hot. When it cooled down, the steel contracted, or got smaller. Would the two pieces of the Arch line up when it was time for the last piece to fit? No one was really sure.

October 28, 1965, was a big day on the Gateway Arch. Workers on each side of the Arch watched as a crane slowly lowered the last piece into place. Huge jacks pushed the two legs of the Arch apart so the final eight-foot piece would fit. When the

The metal support between the arch to keep the legs in place

jacks released, the force of the steel legs held the last piece in place. Then workers bolted the piece in tight.

Although the last piece of the Arch was in place, there was still a lot of work to do. Workers finished the outside of the structure. They finished building the trams. Finally, on July 24, 1967, the first visitors rode one of the trams to the top of the Arch.

However, the Arch was not dedicated until May 25, 1968. Even then, the Arch wasn't finished. Workers still had to complete the grounds of the memorial. A Grand Staircase was built from the Arch down to the Mississippi River. Finally, in 1976, the Grand Staircase was finished. That same year, America's 200th birthday, a Visitor Center and a new Museum of Westward Expansion opened at the base of the monument.

Vice President Hubert Humphrey at the dedication ceremony on May 25, 1968

Catching the Light

The Gateway Arch can look different at different times of day. Because it is made of shiny steel, it reflects sunlight. The Arch also changes color depending on how the sun hits the metal. On sunny days, the Arch looks like a giant mirror.

When the Arch was finished, some people thought it should be lit at night. The National Park Service asked for plans to light the monument. However, the Arch is so tall that it would take too much energy to light it. It would also be hard to place the lights so they did not reflect off the Arch's surface and interfere with planes above. Finally, the Park Service decided to let natural features, such as the moon and the stars, light the monument.

It's a Fact

On a clear day, visitors to the top of the Arch can see for 30 miles.

The morning sun reflects off the stainless steel sides of the Gateway Arch.

"…a soaring curve in the sky that links the rich heritage of yesterday with the richer future of tomorrow."

–Vice President Hubert Humphrey
speaking at the 1968 dedication ceremony

Visiting the Gateway Arch

The Gateway Arch is part of the Jefferson National Expansion Memorial. The Memorial is run by the National Park Service. It is a National Historic Site. That means it is one of America's most important places.

More than one million people visit the Gateway Arch each year. There is a lot to do there. Visitors can walk through the Memorial's park and look at the Arch and the Mississippi River. They can visit the Museum of Westward Expansion outside the statue. Here they can learn about Native American history and the Lewis and Clark expedition. They can also learn about everyday life in the 1800s and find out about the settlers who traveled to the western frontier.

The Arch Store offers Arch-themed souvenirs, books, and gifts.

View from the top of the arch

Of course, most visitors also want to visit the top of the Arch! Each tram can travel to the top of the Arch in four minutes. It takes three minutes to get back down. Once they reach the top, visitors can look out of the windows and get a great view of the city and the river.

The Gateway Arch is an important symbol of America. The Jefferson National Expansion Memorial honors the president who made the United States bigger. It is a powerful symbol of how our nation grew and changed because of the settlers who were not afraid to travel west into a new world.

Glossary

architect: a person who designs buildings and other structures

bedrock: solid rock under the Earth's surface

dedicated: officially opened an important building

expansion: the process of getting bigger

expedition: a journey taken for a specific purpose

federal: having to do with the central government

foundations: bases that support a structure

frontier: an undeveloped area of land on the edge of settled areas

hollow: empty inside

memorial: something built to remind people of an important person or event

migration: movement of people from one place to another

monument: a statue or building erected to commemorate a historical person or event

scaffold: a platform that supports construction workers

tram: a small train made of cars that runs on a system of cables or tracks

Learn More in the Library

Books

Bullard, Lisa. *The Gateway Arch* (Famous Places). Lerner, 2010.

Sipperley, Keli. *St. Louis Gateway Arch* (Symbols of Freedom). Rourke, 2015.

Web Site

Jefferson National Expansion Memorial

www.nps.gov/jeff/index.htm

Index